P9-DBT-430

Mighty Machines

Bombers

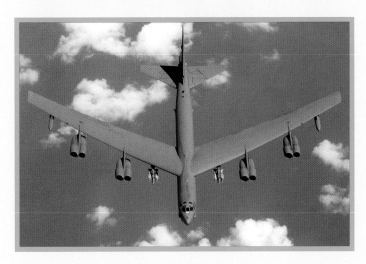

by Jennifer Reed

Consulting Editor: Gail Saunders-Smith, PhD

Consultant: Raymond L. Puffer, PhD
U.S. Air Force Historian
Edwards Air Force Base, California

Capstone
press

Mankato, Minnesota

Pebble Plus is published by Capstone Press,
151 Good Counsel Drive, P.O. Box 669, Mankato, Minnesota 56002.
www.capstonepress.com

1 2 3 4 5 6 12 11 10 09 08 07

Library of Congress Cataloging-in-Publication Data
Reed, Jennifer, 1967–
    Bombers / by Jennifer Reed.
    p.cm—(Pebble Plus. Mighty machines)
    Includes bibliographical references and index.
    ISBN-13: 978-1-4296-0028-6 (hardcover)
    ISBN-10: 1-4296-0028-4 (hardcover)
1. Bombers—Juvenile literature. I. Title. II. Series.
UG1242.B6R44 2008
623.74'63—dc22
                                        2006100702

Summary: Brief text and photographs describe bombers, their parts, and what they do.

Editorial Credits
Mari Schuh and Erika L. Shores, editors; Patrick D. Dentinger, book designer; Jo Miller, photo researcher

Photo Credits
DVIC/MSGT Paul J. Harrington, 4–5; TSGT Richard Freeland, 1, 19
George Hall/Check Six, 8–9
Photo by Ted Carlson/Fotodynamics, cover, 6–7, 10–11, 15, 16–17
U.S. Air Force, 13; Master Sgt. Lance Cheung, 20–21

Note to Parents and Teachers

The Mighty Machines set supports national social studies standards related to science, technology, and society. This book describes and illustrates bombers. The images support early readers in understanding the text. The repetition of words and phrases helps early readers learn new words. This book also introduces early readers to subject-specific vocabulary words, which are defined in the Glossary section. Early readers may need assistance to read some words and to use the Table of Contents, Glossary, Read More, Internet Sites, and Index sections of the book.

Table of Contents

What Are Bombers?

Bombers are big airplanes.
They drop bombs
on targets during battles.

4

Some bombers fly high
in the sky.
They are hard for enemies
to see.

Parts of Bombers

Bombers have fast engines.

Engines push bombers

through the air.

Bombers have computers.

The crew uses computers

to find targets.

The bomb bay holds bombs.

The bay doors open and

bombs drop to the ground.

bomb bay

Bomber Crews

Pilots fly bombers.

A pilot and copilot

sit in the cockpit.

Crew members have

different jobs on bombers.

The navigator tells

the pilot where to fly.

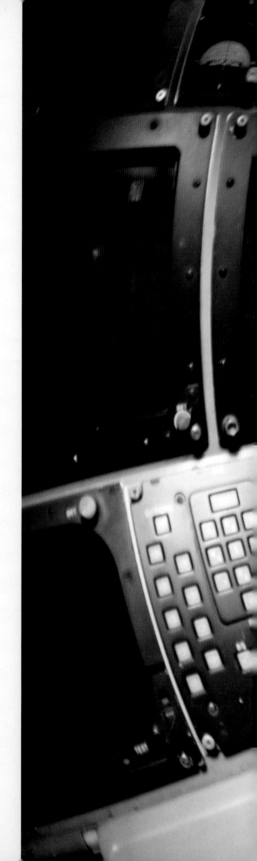

Another crew member

makes sure bombs

hit their targets.

Mighty Machines

Bombers protect the country during battles.

Bombers are mighty machines.

Glossary

battle—a fight between two groups

bomb—an object that blows up when it hits a target

cockpit—the space at the front of an airplane where pilots control the airplane

copilot—a person who helps the pilot fly an airplane

crew—a team of people who work together

navigator—a person who tells the pilot where to fly

pilot—a person who flies an airplane

target—something that is aimed at or shot at

Read More

Braulick, Carrie A. *U.S. Air Force Bombers.* Blazers: Military Vehicles. Mankato, Minn.: Capstone Press, 2006.

Schaefer, Lola M. *Aircraft.* Wheels, Wings, and Water. Chicago: Heinemann, 2003.

Woodward, Kay, and Andrew Woodward. *Aircraft.* Technology All around Us. North Mankato, Minn.: Smart Apple Media, 2006.

Internet Sites

FactHound offers a safe, fun way to find Internet sites related to this book. All of the sites on FactHound have been researched by our staff.

Here's how:

1. Visit *www.facthound.com*

2. Choose your grade level.

3. Type in this book ID **1429600284** for age-appropriate sites. You may also browse subjects by clicking on letters, or by clicking on pictures and words.

4. Click on the **Fetch It** button.

FactHound will fetch the best sites for you!

Index

Word Count: 105
Grade: 1
Early-Intervention Level: 18